I0817412

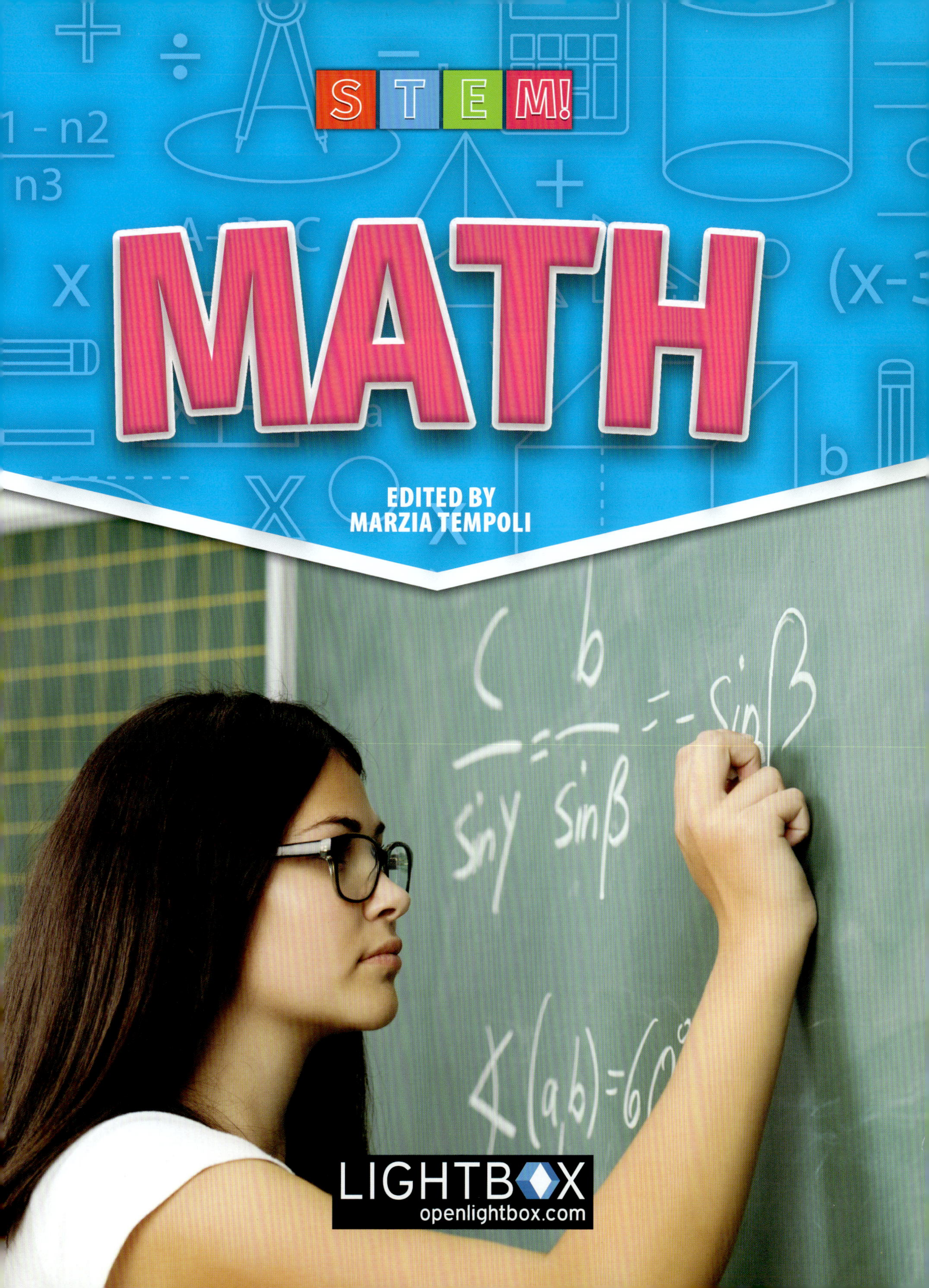
STEM!
MATH
EDITED BY
MARZIA TEMPOLI
LIGHTBOX
openlightbox.com

Go to
www.openlightbox.com
and enter this book's
unique code.

ACCESS CODE

LBXN9788

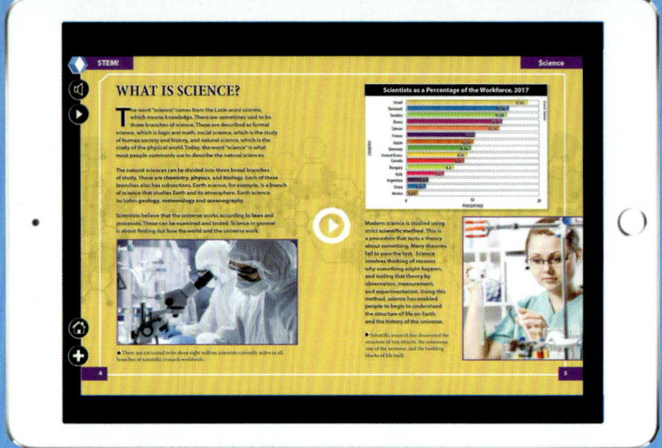

Lightbox is an all-inclusive digital solution for the teaching and learning of curriculum topics in an original, groundbreaking way. Lightbox is based on National Curriculum Standards.

STANDARD FEATURES OF LIGHTBOX

AUDIO High-quality narration using text-to-speech system

ACTIVITIES Printable PDFs that can be emailed and graded

SLIDESHOWS Pictorial overviews of key concepts

VIDEOS Embedded high-definition video clips

WEBLINKS Curated links to external, child-safe resources

TRANSPARENCIES Step-by-step layering of maps, diagrams, charts, and timelines

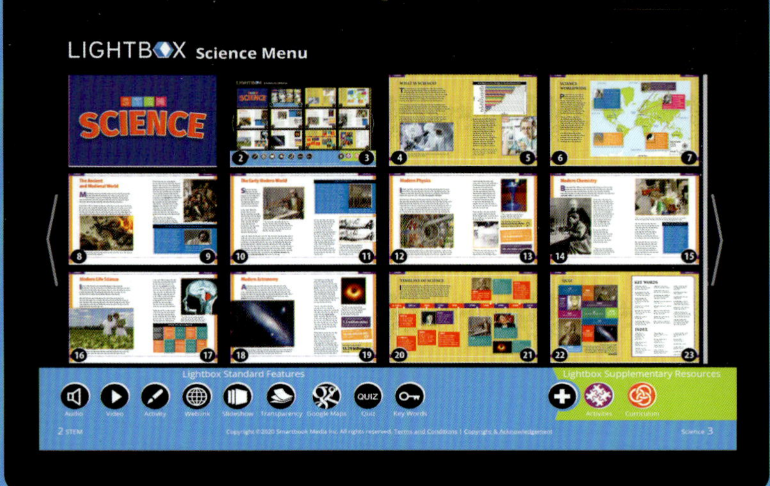

INTERACTIVE MAPS Interactive maps and aerial satellite imagery

QUIZZES Ten multiple choice questions that are automatically graded and emailed for teacher assessment

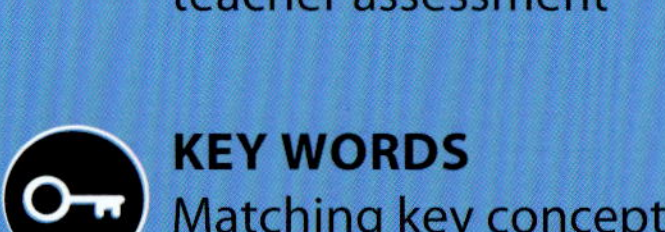

KEY WORDS Matching key concepts to their definitions

MATH

CONTENTS

WHAT IS MATH?

Math is the science of numbers, quantities, and shapes and the relationship between them. Numbers are precise. A farmer in ancient times might have said that his flock of sheep was bigger than his neighbor's flock. Bigger does not mean anything in terms of the number of sheep. Using math to count the sheep, a farmer can say that he has 80 sheep and the other farmer only has 70. The first farmer has 10 more sheep, which proves that his flock is bigger.

Being able to count precisely is not only useful for describing the number of something. It is also used for measuring the passing of time. In ancient Egypt, farmers relied on the seasons to know when to plant crops. They knew that it took 28 days for the Moon to complete one **cycle** from new Moon to full Moon. From this, they were able to predict when the Nile River would flood their fields. Math is also used to work out the relationship between areas. Two rooms may be described as being big, but calculating the area of the floor of a room using numbers shows people which one is actually bigger.

▲ Math, a language that uses symbols and numbers, is a science used in all STEM subjects. STEM stands for Science, Technology, Engineering, and Math.

Mathematicians try to solve problems using logic, or reasoning. The reason why something is true, the proof, helps mathematicians to create general rules. The rules can be used to help solve problems that occur in the real world. People working in business, science, engineering, and construction use math on a daily basis. Math is the underlying basis of art and music, although artists and musicians may not be directly aware of it. Math is also used in activities such as buying groceries or playing computer games. The theories and rules of math help people to enjoy and understand the world.

Branches of Mathematics	
Title	**Description**
Number Theory	Numbers and their relationship to each other
Calculus	The behavior and rate of continuous change, associated with curves and movement
Algebra	Symbols, usually letters, used to work out an unknown number or numbers and the relationship between symbols used in math
Statistics	The collection, analysis, and presentation of numerical data
Combinatorics	Examining the relationship between groups or sets of object or numbers
Probability	Working out how likely something is to happen
Geometry	Flat shapes such as lines, circles, and triangles, or solid objects such as cubes
Logic	Determining whether math theories are true or not by a process of reasoning and **probability**, or cause and effect relationships

MATH WORLDWIDE

Math was first developed in the ancient world. Measurements were made using parts of the body as the units of length or width. Ancient peoples worked out basic addition, subtraction, division, and multiplication. The ancient Greeks made great advances in geometry. Pythagoras was a Greek mathematician. Pythagoras' **theorem**, $a^2 + b^2 = c^2$, is still in use today. This equation describes that in a right-angled triangle, the square of the hypotenuse is equal to the sum of the squares of the other two sides.

Greek math was adopted by mathematicians in the Islamic world during the Middle Ages. Persian and Arab mathematicians created the numerals that are used today.

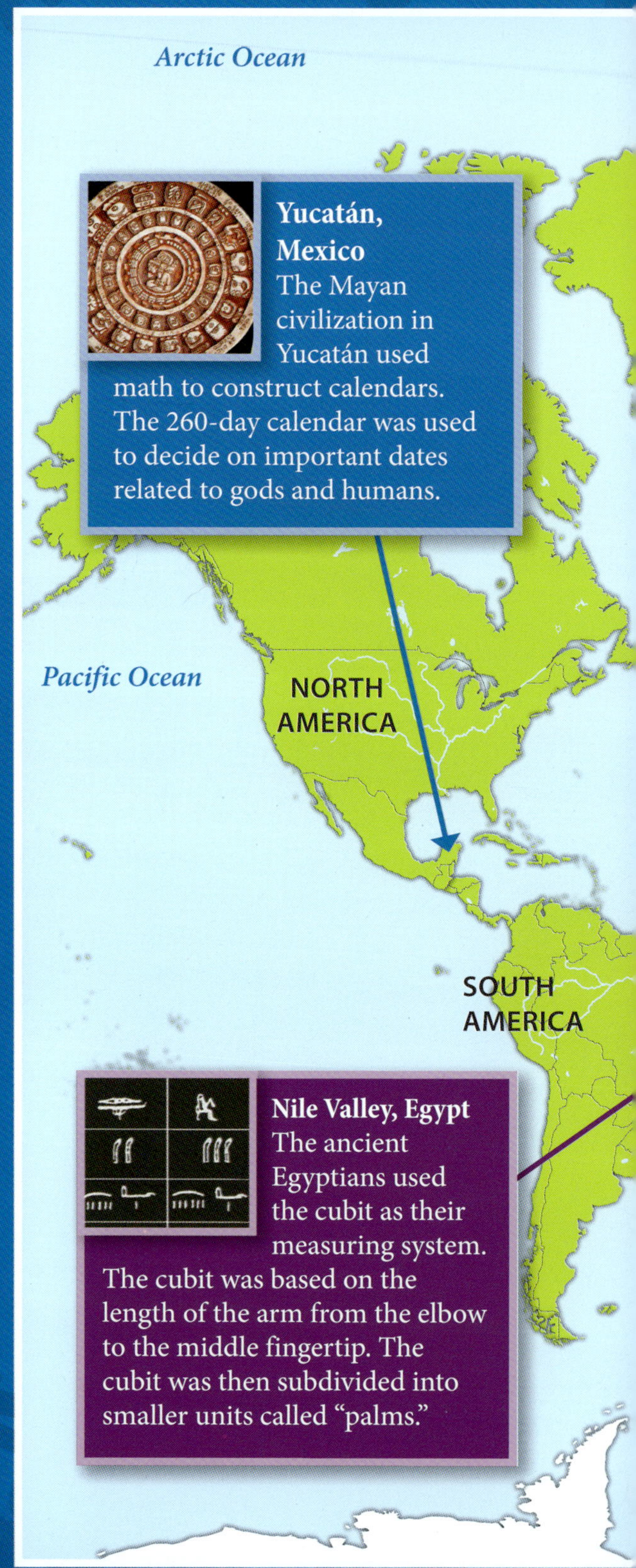

Yucatán, Mexico
The Mayan civilization in Yucatán used math to construct calendars. The 260-day calendar was used to decide on important dates related to gods and humans.

Nile Valley, Egypt
The ancient Egyptians used the cubit as their measuring system. The cubit was based on the length of the arm from the elbow to the middle fingertip. The cubit was then subdivided into smaller units called "palms."

Arctic Ocean
Crotone, Italy
Pythagoras founded a school of mathematicians in the Greek colony of Crotone. They tried to prove that numbers could be used to explain the whole universe.
Baghdad, Iraq
Great thinkers were gathered together by the Caliph of Baghdad, the ruler of the Islamic world. He gave them problems to solve and preserved important Greek texts.
Atlantic Ocean
EUROPE
ASIA
Pacific Ocean
AFRICA
Indian Ocean
Beijing, China
The tradition of math in ancient China used a different number system to that used in the west. The Chinese abacus allowed rapid calculations to be made. It is still used by shopkeepers in the markets of Beijing.
AUSTRALIA
MAP LEGEND
Land
Water
N
SCALE
0
1,000 miles
1,000 kilometers
Southern Ocean
ANTARCTICA

The Ancient World

The oldest known mathematical tool to be found was discovered in 1950 by archaeologists in what is now the Democratic Republic of Congo. The tool was the bone of a baboon, and was named the Ishango bone for the region in which it was found. The bone, dating from about 18,000 BC, is 4 inches (10 centimeters) long and has lines scratched into it. Scientists think these lines are a simple way of counting, or records of the cycles of the Moon, but no one can be sure.

The ancient Egyptians and Babylonians knew how to count, add, subtract, multiply, and divide. They used math to make accurate observations of the skies and to predict certain events such as the movement of the planets. Math enabled the Egyptians to build pyramids with great accuracy. They knew the relationship between different shaped blocks of stone and how to calculate the spaces inside the pyramids. Math also enabled them to create a system of weights and measures.

SYSTEMS OF MEASUREMENT

The ancient Egyptians needed to have a system of standard measurements for use throughout the empire. These measurements were important for instructing people on the size of stone blocks needed to build structures such as pyramids. Egyptian mathematicians invented an official measuring rod called a royal cubit. This could be subdivided into smaller units. Modern measuring rules use a system of numerals, but Egyptian cubit rods were based on symbols. The ancient Romans also had a standard measuring rod. Their cubit was based on the length of the average human forearm. Many measurements used today were originally based on body parts. The 12-inch (30.4 cm) foot was based on the length of a human foot.

▲ Egyptian cubit rods used pictures called hieroglyphs, instead of numbers.

The first ancient Greek math scholar known by name was Thales of Miletus, who invented a theorem about lines and the angles they form within a circle. The Greeks believed that geometry was the most important part of math. Euclid, who worked in the third century BC, was a Greek who lived in Alexandria. He collected what was then known about Greek mathematical theory and wrote it down in 13 chapters of a book called *Elements*. Until the twentieth century, this book remained on the recommended reading lists for math students.

Thales of Miletus lived in the early sixth century BC. He came from what is now the Mediterranean coast of Turkey.

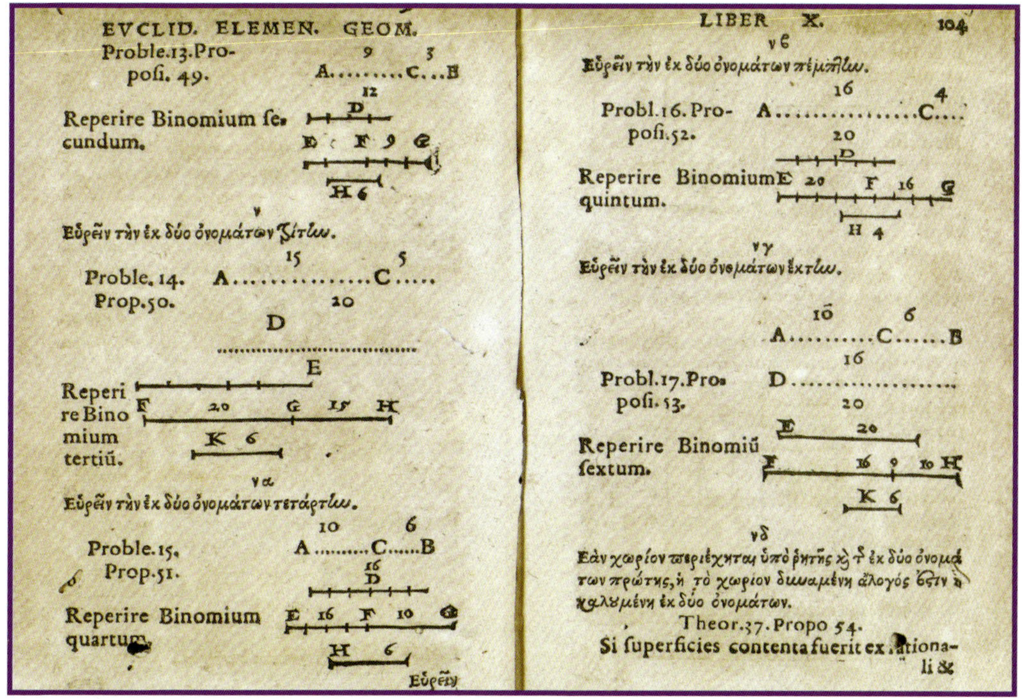

EVCLID. ELEMEN. GEOM.

Proble.13.Proposi. 49. A.........C...B

Reperire Binomium secundum.

ν

Εὑρεῖν τὴν ἐκ δύο ὀνομάτων ἕκτην.

Proble. 14. Prop.50. A...............C.....

Reperire Binomium tertiũ.

να

Εὑρεῖν τὴν ἐκ δύο ὀνομάτων τετάρτην.

Proble.15. Prop.51. A.........C......B

Reperire Binomium quartum.

Εὑρεῖν

LIBER X. 104

νϐ

Εὑρεῖν τὴν ἐκ δύο ὀνομάτων πέμπτην.

Probl.16. Proposi.52. A.................C....

Reperire Binomium quintum.

νγ

Εὑρεῖν τὴν ἐκ δύο ὀνομάτων ἕκτην.

A..........C......B

Probl.17.Proposi. 53. D.....................

Reperire Binomiũ sextum.

νδ

Ἐὰν χωρίον περιέχηται ὑπὸ ῥητῆς καὶ τῆς ἐκ δύο ὀνομάτων πρώτης, ἡ τὸ χωρίον δυναμένη ἄλογός ἐστιν ἡ καλουμένη ἐκ δύο ὀνομάτων.

Theor.37. Propo 54.

Si superficies contenta fuerit ex rationali &

Elements was written in Greek and translated into many languages, including Latin. It was such an important book that, in 1482, it was one of the first math books to be printed after the invention of the printing press.

The Medieval and Early Modern World

In 146 BC, the Romans conquered Greece and made it part of the Roman Empire. The Romans used math for many practical applications. The great roads and buildings of the empire relied on the mathematical discoveries of the Greeks.

▲ The Colosseum was built in Rome in the first century AD. Mathematicians used geometry to plan the stories of parallel arched ovals.

The next major steps forward in the development of math came in India and the Middle East. In India, mathematicians developed different number systems. They also used the idea of zero as a way of showing 10s, 100s, and 1,000s in their calculations. Zero was first used by the Indian thinker Brahmagupta about 628 AD.

Mathematicians in the Islamic world developed these Indian innovations. Al-Khwarizmi worked for the Abbasid Caliph, the ruler of the Islamic world. Al-Khwarizmi was a mathematician at the House of Wisdom, which was the academy of learning in Baghdad. There, he devised a system of numbers based on the numerals from Hindu India. This is the same system of 1, 2, 3 that is used today.

In 1202, Fibonacci, an Italian mathematician from Pisa wrote a book. This introduced the Hindu-Arabic number system to Europe. He showed how these numbers could be used to calculate financial **ratios**, and be a basis for accurate bookkeeping.

In the 1400s, these new numbers became important for calculating distances at sea. European ships had begun to explore the oceans of the world in order to find new trade routes to Asia. Christopher Columbus was an explorer who made four voyages across the Atlantic Ocean. He calculated the size of Earth, although his math turned out not to be as accurate as Greek and Arab mathematicians many centuries before.

In 1543, Nicolaus Copernicus published his theory that the Sun is at the center of the **solar system**. He used math to estimate the movements of the stars and planets. Then, in the 1600s, came a big advance in math. The scientists Isaac Newton and Gottfried Leibniz came up almost simultaneously with the invention of calculus. This made it easier to trace the movement of planets across the skies. It paved the way for further advances in astronomy.

▲Leibniz is credited with inventing calculus in 1684. This was disputed by Newton, who claimed to have had the idea first, but had not made it known.

The circumference of Earth is **24,901 miles** (40,075 km).

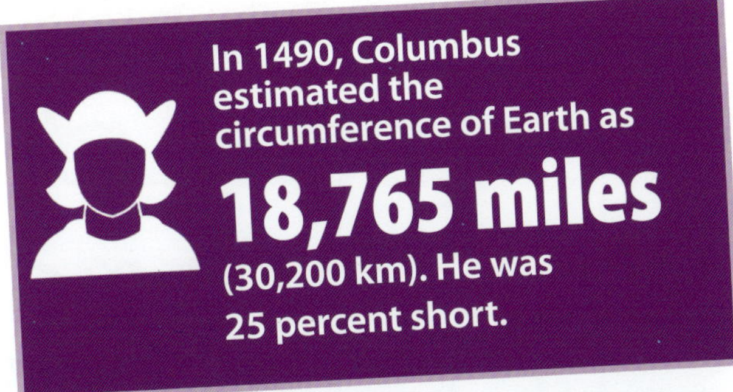

In 830 AD, Islamic astronomers estimated Earth's circumference at **24,000 miles** (38,625 km). They were 5 percent short.

Looking at Numbers

Numbers are the core of math. Today's numbering system has been in use for centuries, and is used every day. People all over the world count 24 hours in a day and seven days in a week. In thinking about money, a shopkeeper knows that $100 is worth twice as much as $50.

However, the system of numbers had to be invented. **Fractions** are an example of this. They are part of a whole number, but the idea of measuring a part of a whole seems impossible. The ancient Egyptians, however, understood the concept of having a part of something that can be divided up. Today, there are two ways that most people calculate parts of a whole. One is by saying, for example, that each part is a quarter of the whole, or that four of these parts fit into the whole. This type of calculation is known as a "vulgar fraction." The second way is to use **decimal places**.

0123456789

٠١٢٣٤٥٦٧٨٩

০১২৩৪৫৬৭৮৯

൦൧൨൩൪൫൬൭൮൯

๐๑๒๓๔๕๖๗๘๙

〇一二三四五六七八九

▲ Several cultures use numeral systems that number from 0 to 9. From top to bottom, they are the Western system, the Eastern Arabic system, the Bengali-Assamese system, the Malayalam system, the Thai system, and the Chinese system.

A useful development in numbers was the invention of the concept of zero. Today, numbers are thought of as a line centered on zero. On one side of zero are the positive numbers, and on the other side are the negative numbers. The symbol +100 on one side of zero is matched by -100 on the other side.

People have devised many aids for arithmetic over the centuries. These include **multiplication tables**. Zero makes adding, subtracting, dividing, and multiplying easier to calculate. This practical application of elementary arithmetic is used by everybody every day. However, another branch of arithmetic, called number theory, is a form of math devoted to the study of numbers. The goal is to find interesting relationships between the numbers themselves. An example of this is prime numbers.

A prime number is one that is divisible only by itself and 1. Every other number can be made by multiplying prime numbers. Prime numbers are important to modern communications. Modern computer security works by using the prime numbers within large numbers. Super-computers are being used to find ever bigger prime numbers, which contain millions of digits.

▲ The 2,000-year-old Tsinghua bamboo strips from China are one of the oldest known examples of a multiplication table.

The largest-known prime number has
24,862,048 decimal digits.

There are **25** prime numbers between 1 and 100.

2 3 5 7 11 13 17
19 23 29 31 37
41 43 47 53 59
61 67 71 73 79
83 89 97

A googol is
10^{100}
meaning 10 followed by 100 zeroes.

10
00000000000000000000
00000000000000000000
00000000000000000000
00000000000000000000
00000000000000000000
00000000000000000000

Looking at Algebra

In the Middle Ages, Al-Khwarizmi wrote a book that gave the first detailed description of algebra. In the book, he described a way of solving equations using letters and symbols as well as numbers. The word "algebra" comes from the name of the book he wrote. The word is also the basis of the word "**algorithm**."

Algebra is used when the exact numbers in an equation or calculation are unknown. Symbols include those for multiplying, dividing, adding, and subtracting. Algebra uses symbols such as those for squaring a number, meaning to multiply a number by itself once. It also uses a symbol for the square root of a number, which is a number that, when multiplied by itself, will give the first number. For example, the square root of 9 is 3.

▲Mathematicians find algebra useful because it allows them to solve equations without having to use numbers. They use symbols to work out unknown numbers.

Algebra is a foundation of math today. In practical terms, it can be used in business to predict sales and calculate the lifetime value of customers to that business. Algebra is also used in computing. In a computer game, the characters are formed by a string of symbols inside the computer. A set of symbols is used to program the software to make the symbols interact. To do this involves the use of algebra.

▲ Al-Khwarizmi's groundbreaking book was explained in writing and described how algebra could be used to solve problems.

FERMAT'S LAST THEOREM

Pierre de Fermat was a French mathematician in the 1700s. After his death, notes he had made in the margin of a book suggested he had found the answer to an algebra problem. This was known as Fermat's last theorem. The problem had first been set by ancient Greek followers of Pythagoras. Fermat's notes said he had found the proof, but there was no space to write it down in the margin. For centuries, other mathematicians tried to solve the problem. The attempts to solve it led to new developments in algebra during the 1800s. In 1993, British mathematician Andrew Wiles produced a paper solving the theorem. When his paper was reviewed, other mathematicians found small inaccuracies in his calculations. Two years later, Wiles published his revised proof of Fermat's Last Theorem. The biggest mystery in math was at last solved.

Looking at Geometry

Geometry is the study of shapes, lines, and angles, and how they relate to each other. The ancient Egyptians used geometry to help them build pyramids and obelisks. They were able to work out the area of shapes such as cylinders, squares, triangles, and polygons. For the Egyptians, geometry was a practical mathematical tool to make construction more accurate.

From about 700 BC onward, the ancient Greeks studied geometry. They used it as a way to understand how the world worked. Some ancient Greeks, such as the followers of Pythagoras, thought numbers found in geometry had spiritual meaning.

Something that Pythagoras and his followers found troubling was that ratios in geometry can result in "**irrational numbers**." These numbers cannot be given as a normal fraction. One of the best known irrational numbers is represented by the symbol π. This is pi, a real number that cannot be specified as a fraction because when calculated in decimal places, the numbers go on without end after the decimal point. Mathematicians call this an "infinite decimal." Pi is the ratio of the **circumference** of a circle to its **diameter**, or the circumference divided by the diameter.

Theories of Greek geometry were collected by Euclid in the third century BC, and for centuries his ideas were unchallenged. In the nineteenth century, however, some mathematicians began to question Euclid's approach. These mathematicians devised what is called non-Euclidean geometry.

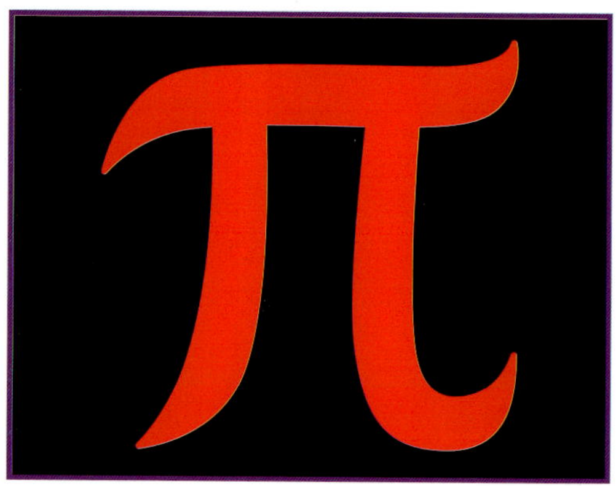

▲The sixteenth letter of the Greek alphabet is used to represent pi. Use of the symbol was made popular by Swiss mathematician Leonhard Euler in the 1700s.

▲ Today, the math behind Mobius strips and other geometric shapes that can be stretched, twisted, crumpled, or bent has practical applications in cosmology, robotics, computer science, and biology.

Euclidean geometry describes objects as flat, two-dimensional planes. Lines are straight, the interior angles of triangles add up to 180°, and two parallel lines never meet. Non-Euclidean geometry looks at shapes and lines in three-dimensions. The Earth is not flat, so the rules of two-dimensional geometry do not necessarily apply.

In 1858, August Mobius, a German mathematician, launched a new branch of non-Euclidean geometry. He discovered a math object that he gave his name to. A **Mobius strip** is a loop with only one side. If the strip is twisted an odd number of times and the ends are fixed together, a line drawn down the center will form a continuous line along both sides of the loop.

π Pi can be simplified as **3.14159.**

Pi has been calculated to **22 trillion** decimal places using computers.

Some people have memorized Pi to **70 thousand** decimal places.

Looking at Statistics and Probability

One way in which math is especially important today is in **statistics** and probability. This area helps people to make important decisions about the way governments, corporations, and households should operate, and how they should use their budgets.

John Arbuthnot was a Scottish doctor who lived in London. He analyzed birth records in the city between 1629 and 1710.

One of the first statistical analyses was by John Arbuthnot. In 1710, he found there were always more boys than girls born per year. He believed that this could not be just chance. In the 1800s, statisticians such as Francis Galton and Karl Pearson carried out research into how likely it was for one individual to be different from a group norm. Anyone differing to a noticeable extent was said to be deviating from the mean.

Today, the math of statistics is important in areas ranging from the analysis of opinion polls to government public health policies. The latest developments in statistical theory have been linked to theories of probability. Computers can be programmed with probabilities and used to make decisions that formerly only a person could make. One example of this is in medical **diagnosis**. It has been shown that properly programmed machines using the math of probability can make many diagnoses better than a doctor. Some people believe that machines will eventually take over many decision-making processes.

WHAT IS AN AVERAGE?

Making sense of statistics is difficult. There are different ways of calculating averages. Three common ways are using "mean," "median," and "mode."

MEAN
The mean value is the number that results when a list of numbers are added together and divided by the total number of numbers. If the list is 2, 7, 9, the numbers add up to 18 and there are 3 numbers. 18 divided by 3 is 6, so 6 is the mean. This is what many people think of when they talk about an "average."

MEDIAN
The median is the middle value when a list of numbers is arranged in size order. In the list 10, 8, 11, 12, 15, the number 11 is in the middle. 11 is the median.

MODE
The mode is the number that appears most often in a set of values. In the list 5, 3, 4, 4, 5, 3, 5, 5, the number 5 appears the most often, making 5 the mode.

▲ Many business people use bar and pie charts to show statistics visually. This makes the results easier to understand in presentations and meetings.

TIMELINE OF MATH

It is not known who first discovered the basic principles of math, but it is known that people were using math many thousands of years ago. Since the Greek mathematicians developed geometry more than 2,000 years ago, math has steadily advanced through the work of many brilliant researchers. Math is the basis of all other sciences, but it is also a world of knowledge in itself. Mathematicians continue to push and test the boundaries of what is possible in order to better understand the universe.

18,000 BC | 300 BC | 500 AD | 1000 | 1200

18,000 BC
People carve lines on the bone of a baboon. It is the earliest known form of calculator.

300 BC
Euclid writes *Elements*. This summarizes all Greek geometry.

628 AD
Indian mathematician Brahmagupta describes the idea of zero.

833
In Baghdad, Persian scholar Al-Khwarizmi completes his book describing algebra.

1202
Leonardo of Pisa, known as Fibonacci, writes his *Book of Calculation*, which introduces the Arabic numeral system to western Europe.

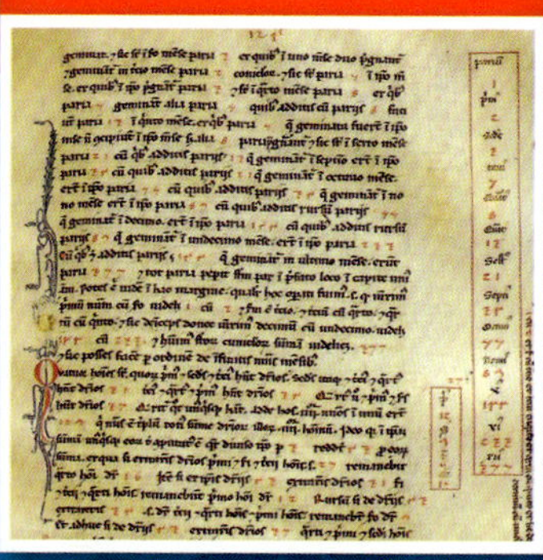

1687
Isaac Newton publishes his paper, *Principia Mathematica*. He calls his discovery of calculus the "science of fluxions."

1900
David Hilbert lists 23 unsolved problems of math. Ten have since been solved.

1995
David Wiles publishes his papers on the proof of Fermat's Last Theorem.

1600 1800 1900 2000 2019

1684
Gottfried Leibniz publishes his paper, *New Method for finding Maxima and Minima,* which describes calculus. It is six pages long.

1798
Carl Friedrich Gauss writes his number theory book, *Disquisitiones Arithmeticae*. It is published in 1801.

2018
The highest yet known prime number is discovered by a computer.

QUIZ

ONE
How long does it take for the Moon to complete one full cycle?

TWO
What was Euclid's collection of books on geometry and math called?

THREE
What part of the body did the ancient Egyptians use as a cubit?

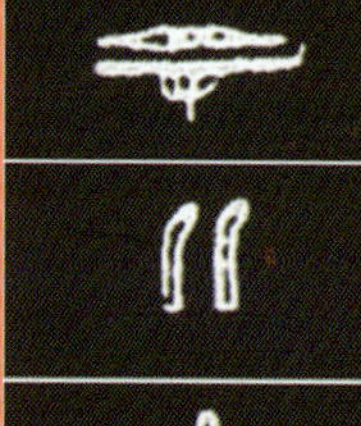

FOUR
Who first proposed the idea of zero in 628 AD?

FIVE
Where was Al-Khwarizmi living when he suggested using Indian numerals?

SIX
Which mathematician introduced the Hindu-Arabic number system to Europe?

SEVEN
Which two mathematicians discovered calculus?

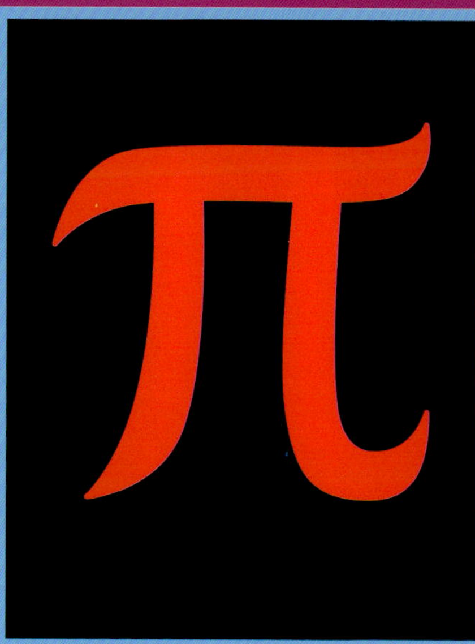

EIGHT
Where did the symbol for pi come from?

NINE
What did John Arbuthnot study?

TEN
What does "mode" refer to when used in statistics?

ANSWERS

ONE 28 days **TWO** *Elements* **THREE** The forearm **FOUR** Brahmagupta **FIVE** Baghdad **SIX** Fibonacci **SEVEN** Isaac Newton and Gottfried Leibniz **EIGHT** It is the sixteenth letter of the Greek alphabet. **NINE** The birth records in London between 1629 and 1710 **TEN** The number that appears most often in a set of numbers

KEY WORDS

algorithm: a set of rules to be followed in a calculation

circumference: the distance around a circle

cycle: a regular repeating pattern

decimal places: ways of showing how something is smaller than a whole number in the decimal system

diagnosis: deciding whether someone has an illness and what the illness is

diameter: the line across the center of a circle

fractions: a way of showing how something is smaller than a whole number

irrational numbers: numbers that cannot be expressed accurately in whole numbers or fractions

Mobius strip: a strip of thin material such as paper that has one edge and one side

multiplication tables: tables that allow people to see quickly the answer to a multiplication calculation

probability: how likely something is to happen

ratios: the relationships between one or more numbers and another number or set of numbers

solar system: the Sun and the planets that go around it

statistics: the analysis of data that has been collected

theorem: a mathematical truth established by proving that something must always be the case

INDEX

LIGHTBOX

SUPPLEMENTARY RESOURCES

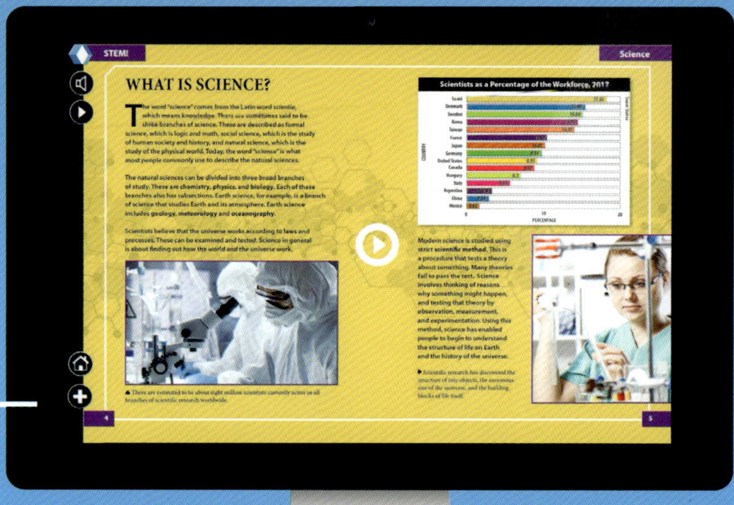

Click on the plus icon found in the bottom left corner of each spread to open additional teacher resources.

- Download and print the book's quizzes and activities
- Access curriculum correlations
- Explore additional web applications that enhance the Lightbox experience

LIGHTBOX DIGITAL TITLES
Packed full of integrated media

VIDEOS

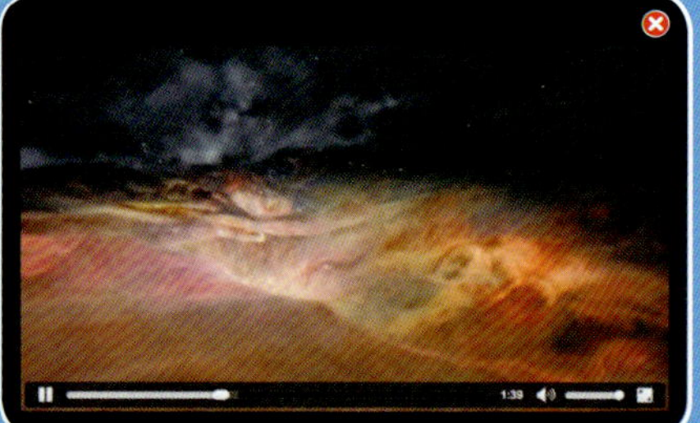

INTERACTIVE MAPS

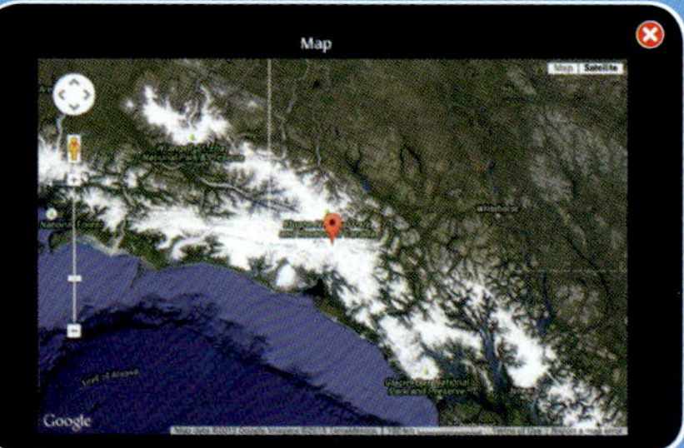

WEBLINKS

SLIDESHOWS

QUIZZES

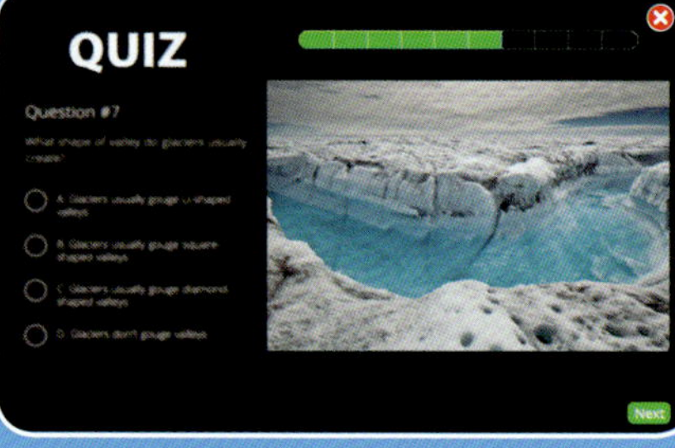

OPTIMIZED FOR
- TABLETS
- WHITEBOARDS
- COMPUTERS
- AND MUCH MORE!

Published by Smartbook Media Inc.
350 5th Avenue, 59th Floor New York, NY 10118
Website: www.openlightbox.com

Project Coordinator: Heather Kissock
Art Director: Terry Paulhus

Library of Congress Control Number: 2019941975

ISBN 978-1-5105-4419-2 (hardcover)
ISBN 978-1-5105-4420-8 (multi-user eBook)

Printed in Guangzhou, China
1 2 3 4 5 6 7 8 9 0 23 22 21 20 19

072019
121819

Photo Credits
Every reasonable effort has been made to trace ownership and to obtain permission to reprint copyright material. The publisher would be pleased to have any errors or omissions brought to its attention so that they may be corrected in subsequent printings.

The publisher acknowledges Alamy, iStock, Shutterstock, and Wikimedia as its primary image suppliers for this title.